My Classroom Poems FOR Young Children

By
Michele Lynn Kilian

along with these Family & Friends:

Louis Kilian (husband)

Patricia Kilian (sister-in-law) & Alan Schwartz (Patricia's husband)

Marlena Wornowicz (sister) & Thomas Wornowicz

Renee Wornowicz (Michele's niece)

Claudia Kellert (sister) & James Kellert

Michael Kellert (Michele's nephew) & Alexa Lewis (Michael's girlfriend)

Barbara Damiano & John Damiano (friends)

Gail Semeniak & Joe Semeniak (friends)

Ellen Haring (friend)

Contents

3	•	Dedication
4	•	Foreword
5	•	Preface

Poems

6 - 21	•	Animals
22 - 25	•	Family & Friends
26 - 28	•	Food
29 - 38	•	Holidays
39 - 44	•	Nature
45 - 51	•	Seasons
52 - 62	•	This 'n That
63 - 66	•	Appendix Tribute Poems

Copyright © 2022 Michele Lynn Kilian along with Family & Friends. All Rights Reserved. No part of this publication may be reproduced or transmitted in any form or by any means without the written permission of the author and contributors.

ISBN 978-0-578-29852-8

Book design by Jaye Medalia

Dedication

This book is dedicated to Michele Lynn Kilian, a 1st and 2nd grade teacher for 39 years who recently passed after a 2+ year battle with cancer. She loved her teaching job, she loved the children and she loved us, her family and friends. Of course, we all loved her. We came together to honor her by sharing one of her teaching tools. She would put a poem a day on the board to start the children's learning day. We thought her approach was unique, so we have a unique way of letting you know how she would feel about this project. We wrote a poem that she would write if she was here with us today.

My Classroom

There is no place like home
Truer words never spoken
But I'll never be home alone
When my classroom door is open

I love all the children
We learn and we play
They get so excited
About my poem a day

And when I see what my family and friends are up to
I pray they don't feel sad
I had a truly wonderful life,
Blessed to be Lou's wife
Please don't any of you feel bad.
I love all of you,
Now go write a poem and paint a happy picture!

Foreword

Throughout her thirty-nine-year teaching career, Michele Kilian implemented many tools and techniques to inspire and enrich her young students. Michele found that poetry sparked the imaginations of children. One of her favorite and effective daily activities was "The Morning Poem." Children read, copied and treasured their morning poems. Michele shared her success with using poetry to stimulate and open the minds of children with fellow teachers who then successfully shared the morning poem routine in their own classrooms.

Michele influenced me to try the poem a day idea. All teachers of young children use poems, but the poem a day strategy is different in that it starts their day off in a way that helps them focus and get ready to learn all day! I tried it and after a week or two, sure enough, the students were asking "Where is our poem today?" if I missed a day.

The poems and illustrations in this book cover a wide variety of topics, all relatable to young children. They can be used by individual teachers as they see fit to meet the needs of their own students, possibly copied into poetry notebooks, as whole class read alouds, or to supplement a current unit, season or holiday. Creative teachers will find many ways to fit these poems and illustrations into their daily lessons. Parents, too, could enjoy establishing a daily poem routine at home with their children.

Michele inspired a love of poetry in her young students. We hope other teachers and families enjoy and use the poems in this book to do the same.

Gail Semeniak
2nd Grade Teacher (retired)

Preface

They say "Teaching is a work of heart." It takes dedication, hard work, planning, passion and innovation to be a successful teacher. Most importantly, a love of your job and your students makes a special teacher who leaves a lasting imprint on the hearts of children. Michele Kilian, known as Mrs. Kilian to her students, was that kind of teacher. She put her heart into all that she did.

Michele had a special way with children. She knew every child in her class well and was close to each one of them. As a result, they came to love and trust her. She instilled kindness. She inspired acceptance. She filled them with knowledge, laughter, and joy. Michele received many honors throughout her thirty-nine-year career, but just as important to her was the love and respect of her students, and watching them thrive both academically and socially.

The point of this preface is to highlight a simple teaching tool that Michele used, "The Morning Poem." She heard from many former students and their parents over the years. They told her how much they enjoyed having her as their teacher and often said that The Morning Poem was one of their favorite activities.

This collection of poetry is an array of imagination and inspiration in verse. Michele simply kept her collection of poems on notecards. She never claimed to be a poet, she was a teacher who effectively used poetry daily in her classroom. All of these poems are original, most written by Michele. Additional poems and illustrations are included that were created by her family and friends in honor of Michele and one of her favorite teaching tools, poetry. This book is also a "work of heart" and we hope it helps other teachers and families touch the hearts of children in their lives, as Michele did.

All illustrators and authors are unpaid volunteers and all net proceeds from this book will be going to The St. Jude Children's Hospital for kids with cancer, where families never pay a cent for their child's care. Michele Kilian died after a 2+ year battle with cancer, all the while keeping her spirits up and thinking of others. This is a final tribute to her belief that we need to look out for others, especially our children.

The Family and Friends of Michele Kilian (Mrs. Kilian)

★ ANIMALS ★

Little Goldfish

Little goldfish
Swimming, splashing
With so much commotion
Do you think
That you are still
Living in the ocean?

poem: Michele • illustration: Barbara

Peacocks Can't Swim!

I lost my peacock named Hank
I took him out to the lake and he sank
I dove around in a circle
And was greeted by a turtle
Who helped me and we both saved Hank!

poem: Lou • illustration: Patricia

Cat Food

Our kitten– we all call him Huey–
Will never eat liver so chewy
Nor the milk, nor the fish
That we put in his dish
He will only dine on chop suey

poem: Michele • illustration: Barbara

Tiger, Tiger

Tiger, tiger
Show your teeth
Grin and roar so loudly
Stand and toss
Your head about
And prowl around quite proudly

poem: Michele • illustration: Patricia

ANIMALS

You Gotta Eat

I met a blue-eyed cow one day,
And not wanting to be rude,
I said "Hi. How do you do?"
And she politely mooed.

She had a flower in her mouth,
She'd chosen from a bunch,
I never could quite understand
The things she liked to munch.

poem: Ellen • illustration: Patricia

The Hummingbird

Searching for red flowers,
From high above the ground,
Hoping when I find some,
There's enough to go around.
Some say I'm aggressive,
But they don't really know
How long until my next meal
I may have to go.

poem: Ellen • illustration: Patricia

Who to Pet and Who Not to

Go pet a kitten, pet a dog
Go pet a worm for practice
But don't go pet a porcupine–
You want to be a cactus?

poem: Michele • illustration: Patricia

ANIMALS

A House for One

The turtle children
Sister and brother
Do not live in one house
With their father and mother
Each baby turtle
Is happy alone
In a snug little house
Of his very own

poems: Michele • illustration: Patricia

Slow Pokes

Turtles are slow
As we all know
But to them it is no worry
For wherever they roam
They are always at home
So they do not have to hurry

Rabbit School Days

I found your old school picture,
You were cute as you could be,
I hung it in my living room
For everyone to see.
Your ears are your best feature,
Eyes, much like a doe,
But it's that teeny little smile
That really steals the show.

poem: Ellen • illustration: Patricia

Dinosaur

I am dinosaur,   I am dinosaur
Hear me roar.   See me romp.
I have wings   I have giant feet
Watch me soar.   Watch me stomp.

poem: Alexa • illustration: Barbara

Martha the Raccoon

Martha is a big raccoon
She has a lot of bustle
To get each trash can upside-down
She really has to hustle
And before the school bus comes
We have to hurry too
And clean up all that trash and stuff
That's spread by you-know-who

poem: Michele • illustration: Marlena

ANIMALS

Plans

When I grow up
I plan to keep
Eleven cats, and let them sleep
On any bedspread
That they wish
And feed them people's tuna fish
poem: Michele
illustration: Barbara

Our Backyard Birds

We love to feed our backyard birds,
It's clear they love it too!
They talk but I can't understand their words
Perhaps they say thank you!
We've got robins and finches
Woodpeckers real big
Chickadees just inches
And a grosbeak who looks like
   he's wearing a wig
poem: Lou
illustration: Marlena

About Fish

A school of fish
Is not a class
It's just a large collection
Of all the fish
With a similar wish
To go in one direction
poem: Michele • illustration: Patricia

A Little Dog

   A little dog
   Not big at all
   A little dog
   To come when we call
   A dog to bark
   And jump and play
   A dog to run
   With us all day
   poem: Michele
   illustration: Renee

ANIMALS

Sleepy Fish

Down in the sea where the fishes sleep
The water is wet
And the water is deep
And all the little fishes keep
Their eyes wide open while they sleep
poem: Michele • illustration: Patricia

I Do Not Laugh

I do not laugh
At a giraffe
Because he's big and tall
I just wish
I could be so high
And not so short and small
poem: Michele
illustration: Patricia

I've Got a 3,000 Pound Cat

I've got a 3,000 pound cat
That isn't much help in my house
The reason is probably that
I've got a 4,000 pound mouse!
poem: Michele
illustration: Barbara

★ ANIMALS ★

Whales
A whale is a mammal
That lives in the sea
A whale has to breathe
Like you and like me
And if I went fishing
For something to cook
I'd not want to catch
A whale on my hook
poem: Michele
illustration: Patricia

Lambs
Lambs are full of curly wool
If they combed it, it would pull
How lucky mother sheep don't care
If their children comb their hair
poem: Michele

The Snake
Don't ever make
The bad mistake
Of stepping on
The sleeping snake
Because his jaws
Might be awake!
poem: Michele
illustration: Patty

A Robin
I wonder how a robin hears?
I never yet have seen his ears
But I have seen him turn his head,
And pull a worm right out of bed
poem: Michele • illustration: Patricia

ANIMALS

Majestic

She glides like a queen
On the River Nile,
Proud and in charge
In regal style.

Her babies struggling
To keep pace
And imitate
Her striking grace.

poem: Ellen

My Cat's Motor

There must be a motor
Inside of my cat
What else could it be
That would sound just like that?
I've learned how to start it
By rubbing her fur
But I've never found out
How to turn off the purr

poem: Michele
illustration: Renee

Walking My Dog

My dog and I are at the beach,
We walk along the sand
He pulls so hard upon his leash
That I can hardly stand.
So as I'm pulled behind him,
I guess it's plain to see,
Am I really walking him,
Or is he walking me?

poem and illustration: Barbara

★ ANIMALS ★

Who are you?
Are you perch or are you koi,
Pretty little fish?
Or maybe for much bigger fish
You're just a tasty dish.
Perhaps you are an angelfish,
I don't think you are a guppy.
But one thing that I know for sure,
You are not a puppy.

poem: Ellen • illustration: Patricia

My Best Friend, The Dog
Strong and smart
 Quick to start
  With speed of a steed
   A friend to the end
    On that you can depend.

poem: Thomas
illustration: Marlena

Little Green Lizard
Little green lizard
Sitting on a stone
Little blond boy
Watching all alone
Quick green movement
Almost like a rocket
Little boy is quicker
Lizard's in his pocket!

poem: Michele
illustration: Barbara

My Dog

His feet are big
His ears are floppy
When he eats
He's very sloppy
He can't do tricks
Jump over sticks
Or anything that's clever
But he's my own
My very own
And I've loved him
Forever!

poem: Michele • illustration: Barbara

ANIMALS

Top Heavy
Colorful as a traffic light,
Red and green and yellow,
This toucan's bill seems way too big
For this little fellow.
Having to tote that bill around,
I'm surprised he can get off the ground!

poem: Ellen • illustration: Patricia

Foxes
Two foxes stopped in our yard
One day last fall they did spend,
They treated each other with
  such regard
I think they were very good friends!

poem: Lou

Painted Bunting
In Florida we did see
A bird as cute as can be
Can this be real?
A bird with red, green, yellow and teal?
Painted Bunting is his name
And he looks to be aflame!

poem: Lou • illustration: Marlena

The Roadrunner
He's a bird that can fly
But he's not good at that.
Yet he runs really fast
Under his feathery hat!
But you better look quick,
He'll be gone lickety split!

poem: Lou • illustration: Patricia

ANIMALS

Monarch Butterfly
The Monarch is a butterfly,
As regal as it's name.
It's easy to identify,
By the color of its frame.
Bright black and orange of body,
Along with white tipped wing.
It has a delicate majesty,
As regal as a king.
poem: Barbara and John • illustration: Barbara

The Heron
A bird appeared back by our creek
Wow - what a wild physique
Longest legs I've ever seen
Maybe she's a queen
Should I toss her a sardine?
Heron was our visitor
So much fun to see her!
poem: Lou • illustration: Patricia

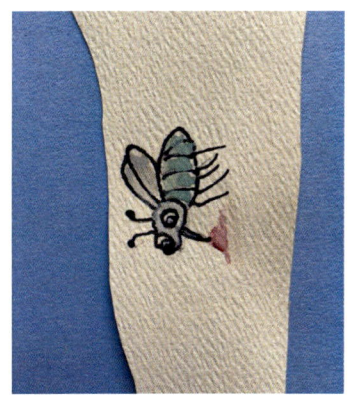

The Oyster Shell
This shell was once an oyster's home
It's smooth inside and shaped like a dome
The owner must have been a rich Duke or Earl
I feel this is true, as he left me this pearl!
poem: Alan • illustration: Patricia

An Itchy Bump
It flew into my room last night,
Very incognito.
It left me with an itchy bump
That nasty, little mosquito.
poem: Barbara and John • illustration: Barabra

ANIMALS

If Only...

If I had eight arms
Like an octopus does,
I'd be more efficient
Than I ever was.

Doing my homework,
Washing the dishes,
Fulfilling each one
Of my parents' wishes.

poem: Ellen • illustration: Patricia

Unwelcome Visitor

We have a bear that visits us
At our house by the lake
With bird food he makes such a fuss
The birds can't catch a break
We hear birds in the trees
Telling him "Go home please!"

poem: Lou

The Woodpecker

Rat-a-tat-tat!
What's that? What's that?
It's a woodpecker tapping on trees
What does it find?
Bugs of all kinds,
Caterpillars, ants, and bees

poem: Michele
illustration: Renee

ANIMALS

Blue Butterfly

I emerged from my cocoon,
One bright and happy day,
Out in the world and all alone,
I had to make my way.
I no longer seemed to be
A caterpillar hairy,
But a wondrous butterfly.
So blue-tiful and airy.

poem: Ellen
illustration: Patricia

If I could be a butterfly

If I could be a butterfly
I think it would be fun
To fly across a flower garden
And land on every one.

poem: Barbara and John

Little Helicopters

Hummingbirds come from
    near and far
Like little helicopters they are
Hang in the air and feed
    right there
Such a sight to see!

poem: Lou • illustration: Patricia

High Jinx

I'd never seen a giraffe
Before my first time to the zoo,
So I went and stood behind the fence
Looking for a clue.
I thought I'd introduce myself,
Said, "What is your name, please?",
Then heard a voice from high above,
"You're talking to my knees."

poem: Ellen • illustration: Patricia

ANIMALS

The Snail

If you look
You will find me,
Just follow my
Silvery trail.
I am slow and
I am slimy,
With my shell
Dragging behind me.

poem and illustration: Barbara

If I Had to Meet a Gorilla

A gorilla is an animal
That's very big and strong
It has a wrinkled raisin face
And arms so very long
If I had to meet a gorilla
I'll tell you what I'd do
I'd meet it in the safest place
I'd meet it at the zoo

poem: Michele
illustration: Barbara

Ducks

When our ducks
Waddle to the pond
They're awkward, as awkward can be
But when they get
In the water and swim
They glide most gracefully

Poem: Michele

Not A Bear At All

At the zoo one day,
From a distance I spied,
What appeared to be a hairy bear
With shoulders oh so wide.
But when he stood so very tall,
I saw something quite familiar.
It was not a hairy bear at all,
But a very large gorilla.

poem: Barbara and John

ANIMALS

A Hoppy Ride

I wish I knew
A kangaroo
Who'd let me hop inside
And join her little joey
On a hop, hop, hoppy ride

poems: Michele
illustration: Barbara

About Rides

I can ride in a car
I can ride in a train
I can ride in a bus
And ride in a plane
But I guess I can never
And neither can you
Ever ride in the pouch
Of a kangaroo

The Kangaroo

It is a curious thing that you
Don't wish to be a kangaroo
To hop, hop, hop
And never stop
The whole day long
And whole night too!

After the Zoo

I like to see what the animals do
Every time I go to the zoo
But then I get to wonder, too
What they all think of me and you

poem: Michele
illustration: Renee

Bears

Bears have few cares
When the wind blows cold
And the snow drifts deep
They sleep
And sleep and sleep
And sleep

poem: Michele
illustration: Patricia

The Owl

It is hard to see this bird,
But his "Hoo-Hoo" can be heard
Follow his sound
He turns his head around!

poem: Lou • illustration: Patricia

ANIMALS

Little Rooster
Little rooster crowin'
Must be something on his mind.
Well I feel just like that rooster
Sunrise can treat me so unkind!
poem: Lou • illustration: Patricia

The Chipmunk
Chitter-chatter, chitter-chatter
Is the chipmunk's steady patter,
Even when he's eating acorns
Which he hopes will make him fatter
poem: Michele • illustration: Marlena

Spoonbill
The spoonbill is a neat looking bird
You can see where he got his name
While it works good for soup
Like a big scoop
It's no help with pizza!
poem: Lou • illustration: Patricia

The Hornet's Nest
I spied a balloon high in a tree,
It piqued my curiosity,
It beckoned to me, come and see,
But my common sense said, let it be.
It must have been my lucky day,
That I had the sense to stay away,
Out of reach, all for the best,
For that balloon was a hornet's nest!
poem: Ellen • illustration: Barbara

ANIMALS

Chickadees!
Chickadees are friendly,
And they land so gently,
They take bird seed from
  your hand
So much fun when they
  land!
poem: Lou

Angelfish
Fish
Tropical, colorful
Swimming, gliding,
  shimmering
Live in coral reefs
Angelfish
poem: Gail
illustration: Patricia

Angelfish
It has many colorful stripes,
And is as flat as a quarter,
But its delicate wings
Make it an angel in water.
poem: John
illustration: Patricia

Two Cats
I have two cats.
One is grey and the other black.
They run around
The house, the yard, I can't
  keep track.
To get them back,
All I do is toss a snack.
poem: Barbara and John
illustration: Barabra

FAMILY & FRIENDS

I Used To Dislike Mornings

I used to dislike mornings
No matter how hard I tried.
But now they're never boring,
And I will tell you why.

We start each day with teacher
Reading us a poem.
We talk about it in our class,
And then we take it home.

poem: Barbara and John • illustration: Barbara

Days For Ones We Love

There is a day for mothers,
One for fathers too.
Even one for grandparents,
But just one day won't do.
So every day I can,
I give them each a hug.
I hold them very closely,
And tell them I love you.

poem: Barbara and John
illustration: Barbara

FAMILY & FRIENDS

My Little Sister

My little sister
Likes to eat
But when she does
She's not too neat
The trouble is
She doesn't know
Exactly where
The food should go

poem: Michele

Freckles

Jerry has freckles
Peppered with spice
And Jerry has a pony
I rode on twice
I think freckles
Are awfully nice

poem: Michele
illustration: Barbara

Big and Little

Long ago, when I was three
Mother looked so big to me
Now I'm six and baby
 brother
Thinks I'm as big as Mother!

poem: Michele
illustration: Barbara

FAMILY & FRIENDS

Walking With Grandpa

Walking with grandpa
On a country road
We find a dotted bug
And a very bumpy toad.
We see a bluebird on a nest,
And a brown hawk flying low,
And a large lacy spiderweb
Swinging gently to and fro.
I'm getting so very tired,
And we could stop this walk I know,
But we have so much more to see
And so many places to go.

poem: John
illustration: Barbara

Grandpa Thinks I'm Funny

Grandpa thinks I'm funny
He laughs at all my puns,
He hugs me and he tells me,
They all are funny ones.
But I tell them to my friends
And they don't really laugh
I think because
   Grandpa loves me
He laughs on my behalf!

poem: John

Sisters

She likes school,
Sometimes I don't.
She does chores,
Sometimes I won't.
She likes chocolate,
Vanilla's what I like.
She's always walking,
While I will ride a bike.
Even though we're opposites,
On this we can agree.
We are the best of sisters,
Best there could ever be.

poem: John

FAMILY & FRIENDS

Hair

My hair is black and curly,
But there's something that
  it needs.
I really like it best,
When Mommy adds some beads.

poem: Barbara and John
illustration: Barbara

Beach Day

The early morning rises,
Our family packs up the car.
Smelling sea salt in the air,
People coming from near and far.
Swimming, surfing, and sand castles
So many fun things to do!
Always counting down the days,
Until we see the ocean blue.

poem: Michael • illustration: Barbara

One Close Friend

If you are blessed
With lots of friends
You might think it best
To have so many gems
While lots are great
One close friend can be
Better than eighty-eight
That I guarantee!

poem: Lou
illustration: Barbara

FOOD

Strawberry Sundae

Have two scoops and eat
This very special treat
Always the real fun way
Is as a strawberry sundae
Whipped cream, don't stop
Add the berry to the top!

poem: Alan
illustration: Patricia

Three Pears

Three pears on a counter
So golden and ripe
Oh how I would love to take a big bite!
I think I will, it would be such a treat
To taste a yummy pear so juicy
 and sweet!

poem: Claudia • illustration: Patricia

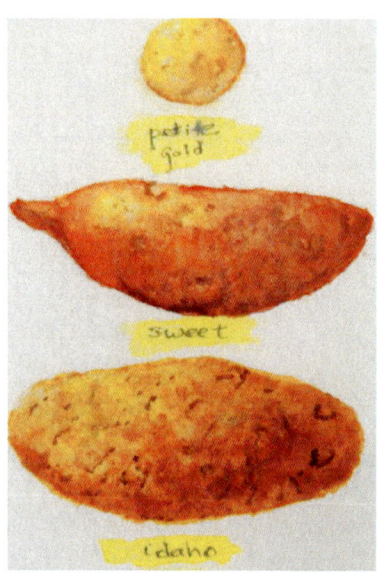

Taters

Beneath the surface, I am told,
You can mine for Yukon Gold.
Not too shiny, covered in mud,
The treasure here is called
 a spud.
My mom so very often tries,
To tempt me with her savory fries,
'Tho others never cease to rave,
The potato chip is still my fave.

poem: Ellen • illustration: Patricia

FOOD

I Love Lemons!

Bright and yellow,
They can be a treat,
But they are not really good to just eat,
Use them to make lemonade
And you won't be dismayed!

poem: Lou • illustration: Patricia

Super Veggies

Mother calls them vegetables
They're always on the table
Some are a lot of fun to eat
Especially mashed potatoes
They'll make you big and strong
While keeping you alert
But the real reason I eat them all
Is ice cream and dessert

poem: Tom • illustration: Patricia

Orange Is A Color

Orange as a color
It sure is hard to beat.
Nothing rhymes with orange,
But they sure are good to eat.

poem and illustration: Barbara and John

Potato Wedges

Small potato wedges,
Crisp, brown, golden edges,
Seasoned to perfection
A beautiful collection.
Sizzlin' hot, delicious,
My hunger pangs are vicious.

poem: Ellen • illustration: Patricia

★ FOOD ★

Full Meal
While dining, a Nanny goat said,
Don't bring me the salad and bread
For what I like best
Is a bit of wool vest
And a shirt
And a tie that is red
poem: Michele • illustration: Patricia

Lemon Meringue Pie
Mom made a lemon pie and went
   next door
My brother and I went to taste it
We couldn't stop, we wanted more
Mom came home and we had to say
"Mom we ate your pie today!"
poem: Lou • illustration: Patricia

Half Happy
A worm in the
   apple, they say
Was ever so happy that way
Till a fellow named Dapple
Bit into the apple
The worm was half happy that day
poem: Michele • illustration: Patricia

Hot Fudge Sundae
I'd love to have a hot fudge sundae
Not just on Sunday, but any
   day with a y
Maybe I can make one myself one day
Maybe today's the day to try!
poem: Lou • illustration: Patricia

HOLIDAYS

Jack O'Lantern
They cut off the stem
On the top of my head
And to the birds
My seeds were fed.
They carved me out
This toothy face
And placed me
In this window space.
poem and illustration: Barbara

Father's Day
Father's Day is the special day,
But not the only day,
That I say to my Daddy
How much I love him
For all he means to me.

poem: John
illustration: Patricia

Martin Luther King Jr.
Martin Luther King
Led the March on Washington.
He spoke about his dream
That all could live as one,
That children of all colors
Could live within a land,
Where they could play together
Walking hand in hand.

poem: Barbara and John
illustration: Barbara

HOLIDAYS

On Halloween Night

A witch swept a cloud
Into Mr. Moon's eye
Blink went the moon
Black went the sky!

Then down on a post
A pumpkin head, bright
Did Mr. Moon's job
On Halloween night

poem: Michele • illustration: Patricia

GroundHog Day

The groundhog came out
Of his hole today
To see what he could see
He saw his shadow
And went back in
More winter for you and me

poem: Michele • illustration: Patricia

The Holidays

The holidays are almost here
Time for family and friends to
   spread good cheer
Joyful music, fun gifts, and good
   times we'll recall
Makes the holiday season the
   merriest of all!

poem: Claudia • illustration: Tom

HOLIDAYS

The Riddle

Leprechaun, leprechaun
Under a tree
I know you're hiding
Your hat from me
Leprechaun, leprechaun
Where is your hat?
I can't tell, I can't tell
I can't tell you that

St. Patrick's Day

A little merry sunshine
A little wind at play
And lots and lots of green
All for St. Patrick's Day

Valentine's Day

Today is Valentine's Day
With hearts and cards and candy
I give a Valentine to you
And hope you have one handy

This page poems: Michele • illustrations: Patricia

Thanksgiving Day

Thanksgiving day
Is here again
And all the children shout
Hurrah for turkey
Me-oh-my
For cranberry sauce
And pumpkin pie
Thanksgiving is here at last!

Thanksgiving Weather

Outside the wind is sharp and cold
It really doesn't matter
Because the pumpkin pie is baked
And turkey's on the platter
The table's set, we've gathered round
We all sit down together
With such a fine Thanksgiving feast,
Who frets about the weather?

HOLIDAYS

Red, White and Blue

The red of the rose,
The white of the snows
The blue of the skies above
These colors there
Are the ones we see
In that flag of the land that we love

poem: Michele • illustration: Renee

Memorial Day

On Memorial Day
In peaceful May
We honor our soldiers
The Blue and the Gray
And other brave men
Who died for us
And kept our country
Victorious

poem: Michele • illustration: Patricia

Remembering Day

All the soldiers marching along,
All the children singing a song
All the flowers dewy and sweet
All the flags hung out in the street
Our hearts throb in a grateful way
For this is our Remembering Day

poem: Michele
illustration: Patricia

Juneteenth

In Texas 1865
Was posted a decree,
Which notified the citizens
That the slaves were free.
We celebrate each year in June
The slaves' emancipation,
A reminder that our goal remains
A free and equal nation.

poem: Ellen
illustration: Gail

HOLIDAYS

Invitation

If I should invite you
For pickled eggs
And chocolate soup
And dragon legs
And peanut stew
To eat in school
Just be prepared
It's April Fools!

poems: Michele
illustration: Patricia

April First

It's April first
A time for fun
I wonder can
You trick someone?
But just watch out
Your friends are quick
Instead of gifts
Watch for a trick!

Easter Egg Hunt

My parents hid eggs
Around our backyard
But we never got to find them
Because we had a big
 St. Bernard
He had a nose for the eggs
And he had a big stomach
 to boot
We couldn't catch him
But boy, what a hoot!

poem: Lou • illustration: Patricia

The Fourth

Dogs on the grill,
Kids can't sit still.
Red, white and blue
Everywhere, too.
Bands in the park
'Til long after dark.
Fireworks popping,
Fun never stopping.
You cannot deny
It's the Fourth of July.

poem: Ellen • illustration: Patricia

Flags are flying
Red, white and blue.
Happy birthday America
We all celebrate you!

poem: Gail

HOLIDAYS

The Search

I thought I'd search the closet
I had to find the box
I couldn't open one door
Cause all the doors had locks
I know I saw the box there
What's in it I can't say
I don't think I will find out
Until sometime Christmas Day

poem: Michele

★ HOLIDAYS ★

Waiting
A tree all dressed
In colors bright
Sparkling and glowing
Alone in the night
Waiting for crowds
To gather around
And make a musical
Holiday sound

Happy Holidays
Holiday lights and holiday
    sights
Holiday gifts bringing cheer
Each in its way, coming
    to say
"Let's have a wonderful
    year!"

Do Rabbits Have Christmas?
Do rabbits have Christmas
I wonder, I wonder?
They have little fir trees to celebrate under
But do they have secrets
And smiles on their faces?
Let's go put some carrots
In rabbit-y places!

I'd Like to Be Like Santa Claus
I'd like to have his beard
And his roly-poly nose
I'd like to drive his sleigh
And wear his furry clothes
I'd dive down chimneys
And never get stuck
I'd bring special goodies
And lots of Christmas luck

This page poems: Michele • illustrations: Patricia

HOLIDAYS

Cinco de Mayo

Celebrating a major victory,
People gather in the streets.
Honoring the red, white, and green,
Along with providing good eats.
The fiesta is grand
With parades and food galore!
Friends and family in Mexico
Remembering the war.

poem: Alexa • illustration: Barbara

Christmas Eve

As I stood on the stairs
This last Christmas Eve,
I looked and saw something
I couldn't believe.
It was Dad in his robe
And unslipperred feet
Eating the cookies
Left for Santa to eat.
He looked very confident,
He must think he's the boss,
But wait until next year
When I tell Santa Claus.

poem: John
illustration: Barbara

Labor Day

Don't you think it's kind of odd,
With a name like LABOR Day,
That you wouldn't have to go to work,
Could enjoy a holiday?
Then all the other work days
When you labor all day long,
Should be known as lazy days,
Do you think that I am wrong?

poem: Ellen • illustration: Barbara

HOLIDAYS

Columbus Day
Christopher Columbus discovered America
On October 12, 1492.
Columbus Day celebrates his arrival
And all of us do too
poem: Barbara and John • illustration: Barbara

Kwanzaa Feast
Kwanzaa is a special time
We gather foods to eat
From the land of Africa
Fruit and nuts and stews and sweets
Happy Kwanzaa!
poem and illustration: Patricia

Mother's Day
I made some paper flowers
For Mom on Mother's Day.
To show her that I love her
On each and every day.
They may not have a pretty scent
Or name you can remember,
But just like my love for Mom,
They will last forever.
poem: Barbara and John • illustration: Barbara

poem: Lou • illustration: Gail

President's Day
President's Day is here
We give thanks and cheer
For Washington and Lincoln
Because it's very clear
Without them, the USA
would not be here!

HOLIDAYS

Hanukkah

Dreidels spinning all around,
Soup and latkes will be found.
Eight whole days to celebrate?
Wow, Hanukkah is really great!

poem: Alexa
illustration: Barbara

poem: Barbara and John
illustration: Barbara

Sunday Tradition

Every Sunday we all go
To Grandma's house for lunch.
My mom and dad, brothers and sisters,
Aunts and uncles and cousins,
The entire bunch.
Every Sunday we all go
To Grandma's house for lunch.

poem and illustration: Barbara and John

The Easter Bunny

Hopping, hopping, hopping,
To hide his Easter eggs.
How does he hop so quickly?
He has such little legs.
But one thing that truly puzzles me
Beyond those little legs,
Is that an Easter Bunny
Could lay all those Easter eggs.

NATURE

poem: Ellen

Sunflowers

Bowing their heads,
Upturning their faces,
Growing unchecked
In wide open places.

Yellow and brown,
On spindly stalks,
Providing the background
Where Michele walks.

A Blizzardy Day

It's snowing! It's snowing!
A fierce wind is blowing!
It's really a blizzardy day!
The snow drifts are piling,
But I'm inside… smiling
And here's where I'm going to stay!

poem: Michele • illustration: Patricia

The Quiet Snow

All this sky
Of falling snow!
All this motion,
All this show
All this stir
And not a sound
In the air
Or on the ground

poem: Michele
illustration: Patricia

NATURE

When I Was Younger

When I was younger
I used to say
The moon is ever
So far away

But men have walked
On the moon, and so
It isn't too far
For me to go

poem: Michele • illustration: Renee

Little Yellow Riddle

Little yellow flowers
Sprout everywhere and grow
And when they puff
And go to seed
They're fun to blow
What are they?
(Dandelions)

poem: Michele
illustration: Patricia

Mt. Etna

There is a volcano in Italy
She is on the island of Sicily
Mt. Etna is her name
Lava and smoke are her claim to fame!

poem: Lou • illustrator: Patricia

Bare Feet

Take off my shoes
Pull off my socks
Feel the funny, knobby rocks
Walk through the grass
Watch out for glass
Let the little spiders pass
Stand where it's cool
Peek in the pool
It's summertime, and no school

poem: Michele

NATURE

Snow

Snow is so white
And crystally clear
It shines like a diamond
When sunshine is near

poem: Michele

Never Mind the Rain

Never mind the rain!
It doesn't leave a stain
Never mind the snow!
It melts before you know
But rain and snow together!
That's pretty nasty weather

poem: Michele • illustration: Barbara

Wind

Wind tossed my hat
Tore my kite
Rattled windows every night
Wind cleared the skies
Brought the sun
So we'd know that
Winter's done

poem: Michele
illustration: Patricia

NATURE

Flowers

Colorful and bright,
So delicate and simple,
Always beautiful.

poem: Alexa • illustration: Barbara

Yellow

Yellow is the color of the sun
The feeling of fun
And I guess
Yellow's the color
Of happiness

poem: Michele • illustration: Patricia

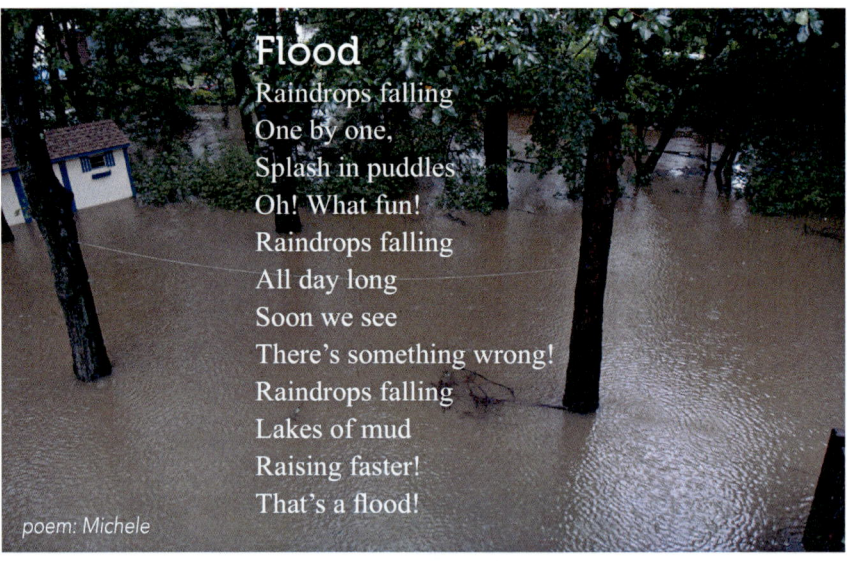

Flood

Raindrops falling
One by one,
Splash in puddles
Oh! What fun!
Raindrops falling
All day long
Soon we see
There's something wrong!
Raindrops falling
Lakes of mud
Raising faster!
That's a flood!

poem: Michele

NATURE

The Friendly Dark
The friendly dark
Just fills my room
When I'm in bed at night
It creeps on tiptoe
All around
To take the place of light
poem: Michele

Stars
Stars in the sky
Twinkling at night
So far yet so bright
Who turns you on at night?
poem: Joe

illustration: Patricia

First Up
Opening for business,
At the crack of dawn,
The morning glory's first to bloom
And beautify my lawn.
So delicate and pretty,
Yet on a hardy vine,
The morning glory promises
That everything is fine.
poem: Ellen
illustration: Patricia

The Sun
The sun came up
In the east today
A blazing yellow sphere.
It crossed the sky
Into the west
And then it disappeared.
poem and illustration: Barbara

NATURE

Petunias

Petunia is a pretty flower
That loves to have a shower
Hummingbirds love
To visit from above
To drink their nectar
With their built-in collector!

poem: Lou • illustration: Patricia

Weeds

Yesterday I pulled the weeds,
I was really in there,
Who knew that today it'd seem
Like I hadn't even been there.
There are many different ways
To mount a strong attack,
But no matter what you do,
The weeds keep coming back.

poem: Ellen • illustration: Patricia

A Study in Color

At first I saw three colors,
Not counting black or white,
But I looked a little closer
At this very pretty sight.
What I saw surprised me,
Lovely green and blue,
And indigo and violet
Like tiny drops of dew.
A really clever artist,
Has made it very clear
That all colors of the rainbow
Are represented here.
Gorgeous!

poem: Ellen
illustration: Patricia

Pretty Blue Flower

poem: Lou
illustration: Patricia

What a pretty blue flower
I wonder what it is
What a quiz
I'm not a whiz
I give up,
It's not a buttercup,
Now I can acclaim
Hydrangea is her name!

SEASONS

That's July

A bunch of grass,
   a wild rose
A bird that's learned to fly,
Children out for holiday
That's July!

poem: Michele
illustration: Patricia

Can't Wait For Summer

I can't wait for summer
When the sun is shining bright.
I'll go down to my favorite beach,
And fly my yellow kite.
I'll dig my toes into the sand,
Building a castle with a moat.
I'll catch minnows with my hands,
And go fishing in a boat.

poem: Barbara and John
illustration: Barbara

Seashells & Lemonade

Trading seashells at the beach
Eating cherries or a peach
Drinking ice cold lemonade
Reading stories in the shade
Playing games in the sun
Summer days can be such fun!

poem: Michele
illustration: Marlena

SEASONS

Summer Is

Summer is picnics
Days at the beach
Summer is ice cream
Chocolate and peach

Summer is sunshine
Kids playing ball
Summer's my favorite
Season of all

poem: Michele • illustration: Patricia

July Again

July again! July again!
School days have gone by again!
Longer sunny days again
For fun in summer ways again
Swim and run and climb again!
Watermelon time again!
Vacation, keeping cool again
Until it's time for school again!

poem: Michele • illustration: Patricia

On Summer Days

On summer days I'd like to be
A walrus in the frozen sea
I think it would be very nice
To play "I Spy" through
   holes of ice

poem: Michele
illustration: Patricia

SEASONS

November
Lovely are the silent woods
On crisp November days
When the leaves fall red and gold
About the quiet ways

poem: Michele • illustration: Patricia

Autumn Shakes
Daddy rakes, while Mommy bakes
The wind whistles through the trees
Leaves are brown, they cover the ground
And the trees shake in the breeze
Summer's gone, a sinking heart
School is just about to start

poem: Thomas • illustration: Anya

Hello Spring
Winter is gone
With its ice and snow
And now its off
To the park we'll go
To race, to skate
To slide, to swing
And shout loud
"Hello" to spring.

Change in the Weather
I think it would be
very good
To have some snow
and sleet
In summer when
We need it most
To drive away the heat

poem: Michele

poem: Michele
illustration: Barbara

SEASONS

Spring River

The ice is melting
On the river
I can see
The water shiver
Like a cold snake
In the sun
Warming up
When winter's done.

poem: Michele • illustration: Patricia

No Drip of Rain

It rained on Ann
It rained on Dan
It rained on Isabella
But it did not rain
On Mary Jane
She had a huge umbrella

poem: Michele • illustration: Marlena

April Showers

Down my face and on my tongue,
Dripping, dripping, dripping.
Jumping in puddles,
Splashing, splashing, splashing.
All fun, fun, fun,
On a rainy April day.

poem: Barbara and John

SEASONS

Springtime

I like springtime.
Lots of showers, then flowers.
But all of a sudden,
It's followed by pollen.
What am I to do - ACHOO!!

poem: Barbara and John
illustration: Barbara

Runny Nose

It's just not funny
When your nose is runny
You feel all soggy
Hoarse and froggy
Your throat is scratching
The germs are hatching
You know it's catching
KERCHOO!

poem: Michele

Signs of Spring

Flowers pushing through the ground,
Chirping birds all around,
Light breeze tickling my face,
Strong winds tearing up the place.
All are signs that Spring is near,
I can't wait 'til it gets here.

poem: Ellen
illustration: Barbara

All About April

Showers, puddles, rainbows, sun
Green surprises
Springtime fun
Robins singing
Tulips out
That's what
April's all about!

poem: Michele • illustration: Patricia

SEASONS

I Built a Snowman

I built a snowman five feet tall
But then the sun came out
Now he's only three feet tall
With puddles all about.
I went to find him later
But all that could be found
Were a carrot and two sticks
And his hat upon the ground.

poem and illustration: Barbara

A Frosty Problem

I like the frosty winter air
And when the cold wind blows
My hands keep warm in mittens
And boots help warm my toes
But I can't think of any way
How I can warm my nose!

poems: Michele
illustration: Patricia

A Snowball

Make your fingers a
   scooper
And scoop up snow
Pack it
Round it
Pack it
Round it
Back your arm and throw!

Winter Time

Winter time, winter time
When everyone gets all cozy.
Cold weather and the fluffy snow
Make our cheeks nice and rosy.

poem: Alexa

Snowy Sidewalk

We watched our walk
Fill up with snow
It looked so soft and smooth!
And then the paper boy
   walked by
And gave our walk a groove

poems: Michele • illustration: Patricia

SEASONS

I Like Snow Days

I like snow days
Always so much fun,
Slipping and a-sliding

Falling as we run.
Building snowmen,
Throwing balls,

Sledding in the park,
Sorry that it had to end
Because it's getting dark!

poem and illustration: Barbara

Winter Blast

Winter is here
look at all the snow!
We'll hop on our snowmobiles
and away we go!
The lake is frozen
we go far and fast!
Winter is here
and we're having a blast!

poem: Gail • illustration: Marlena and Tom

Ice

Ice is nice
If you're straight
As a willow
But much too hard
To use as a pillow

poem: Michele

THIS 'N THAT

The Painting Lesson

Red and blue make purple
Yellow and blue make green
Such a lot of colors
To paint a lovely scene
Pink and blue make orchid
Black and white make gray
Now I'll dry my brushes
Until another day

poem: Michele • illustration: Patricia

Can't Find My Glasses

I dragged myself out of bed
Looked all around the place
I thought my glasses fell on the floor
I couldn't see a trace
Many minutes and time went by
Til they showed up again
Mom found them, and she said,
"Your glasses are on your head!"

poem: Tom • illustration: Barbara

Playing Ball

Ball, ball hit the wall
Hurry back before
  you fall
Hurry back to me,
  and then
I will throw you out
  again

poem: Michele
illustration: Barbara

Nessie

In Scotland causing distress
Is the Monster of Loch Ness
Nessie is elusive
She's very reclusive
As sly as can be
That's how she stays free!

poem: Alan • illustration: Patricia

★ THIS 'N THAT ★

First Thoughts
It's morning– comes the sun
A time for work
A time for fun
A time to finish things begun
A time to smile, a time
   to plan
A time to say, "I know I can!"

poems: Michele • illustration: Patricia

Start the Day
Start the day by dancing
While you sing a little song.
Both will make you happy
All day long.

poem: Barbara and John
illustration: Barbara

Weekends
Vacation is done, school is in
I know just how my day begins
Brush my teeth, comb my hair
After sitting in the breakfast chair
Give mom a kiss, get on the bus
In my bag, pencils and pens
With any luck, I won't be stuck
Hoping for the weekends

poem: Tom • illustration: Barbara

Last Day of School
June has finally come,
Some of the kids are very glum.
The rest are excited and ready to be done,
It's time for fun in the hot, hot sun!

poem: Alexa • illustration: Barbara

THIS 'N THAT

Books

Some books are full of pictures
Some books are very small
Some books are thin
And some are thick
If I were asked
To answer quick
I'd say, "I like them all."

The Library

I know a place
That is filled with fun
It has some things for everyone
It's doors are open
To you and me
The name of the place is the
Library

poems: Michele

The Three "R's"

Reduce, reuse, recycle
Are words that help us
  know
We want to keep Earth
Clean and green
No matter where we go

poem: Michele

Sliding

Down the slide
We ride, we ride
Round we run, and then
Up we pop
To reach the top
Down we come again

poem: Michele • illustration: Barbara

THIS 'N THAT

A Shiny Penny
I found a shiny penny
Lying on the ground.
Dad said it must mean
I'm the luckiest kid around.
It's only made of copper,
It isn't worth too much,
But I will keep it anyway,
It's worth a lot in luck.
poem: Barbara and John • illustration: John

Home
Home is a place to sleep
  and eat
Home is a place to share
And if it's a place
That is warm with love
A home can be anywhere
poem: Michele
illustration: Patricia

A Penny
I have a penny
A penny to spend
I have a penny
A penny to lend
I have a penny
A penny, oh my!
I have a penny,
But what will it buy?
poem: Michele

poem: Ellen

Shore Thing
A day at the shore
Is what I'm longing for,
A week or a month,
I'd like even more.

Sun on my face,
White, foamy lace,
Oh, how I love
This wondrous place.

Wind in my hair,
Salt in the air,
There's no doubt at all
Why I keep going there.

THIS 'N THAT

Baseball

Come grab a ball
A bat and glove
Then join in the game
We truly love
Out at the ball field
You'll hear the call
As the umpire and fans all shout
"Play ball!"
poem: Michele

On the Diamond

Walking through the ballpark,
Lights so big and bright.
What great seats we have,
For homeruns and cheers tonight.
poem: Michael

Crayons

Crayons, crayons
Smell just like wax.
They come
In different sizes
And multi-colored packs.

poem and illustration: Barbara

THIS 'N THAT

Unwelcome
Litterbug, litterbug
Please stay at home
With your trail of trash
Wherever you roam
Visit our parks and benches less
For wherever you go
You leave a mess!

Don't Litter
Don't litter the park
Don't litter the street
Pick up your toys
Keep the world neat
Put trash in the can
Close the lid tight
Don't be a litterbug
Litter's a sight!

poems: Michele • illustration: John

A Big Western Plant!
There is a plant out west
With sharp needles it is dressed
It can be 50 feet high
With arms raised to the sky
Over 200 years old
A sight to behold
Saguaro is a cactus
Good thing they can't attack us!

poem: Lou • illustration: Patricia

Questions and Answers
Questions need answers
And answers need questions
The two go together
They're seldom apart
When children ask questions
They've got to get answers
If they don't get answers
How will they get smart?

poem: Michele • illustration: Barbara

THIS 'N THAT

Recess time is fun and games
Time to run around
After sitting still all day
My feet just hit the ground
Off to play with my friends
Games of skill and art
Doing all the fun things
I love when recess starts!
poem: Tom
illustration: Barbara

I Spy

Find a butterfly
Find a bear
Find a top hat
In the air!

Look for objects
On all the pages
There's plenty of fun
For kids of all ages

poems: Michele • illustration: Patricia

My New Friend

Need a friend?
Find a rock, I say,
Go ahead and laugh, you may.
But in my pocket, he will stay.
poem: Tom
illustration: Barbara

Golf

Daddy and Mommy playing golf together
Daddy is good, but Mommy is better
While Dad can't seem to find his ball
Mom putts hers into the hole

poem: Tom • illustration: Patricia

THIS 'N THAT

Wiggly Tooth

Once I had a little tooth
That wiggled every day
When I ate and when I talked
It wiggled every way
Then I had some candy
A sticky, taffy roll
Now where my wiggly tooth was
Is nothing but a hole!

Guess What?

What can crunch
And what can bite?
And what can gnaw and chew?
What needs brushing
Every night?
Tell us quickly!
Do!
(teeth)

poems: Michele • illustration: Barbara

Mommy's Robe

Mommy wears an old blue robe
Made of fluffy terry cloth.
It's so soft and smells so good
I hold it when she takes it off.

poem: Barbara and John • illustration: Barbara

Keepsakes

I keep bottle caps
I keep strings
I keep keys and corks
And all such things
When people say
"What good are they?"
Their answer's hard to get
For just how I will use them all
I don't know yet

poem: Michele • illustration: Marlena

THIS 'N THAT

Bubbles

Stretching, swelling
Growing, round
Swaying, swinging
Not a sound
Floating, bouncing
  in the air
Bubbles, bubbles
  everywhere

poem: Michele
illustration: Patricia

The Quest

Right on time the tide
  rolls out,
I up and grab my pail,
I'm looking for some
  special shells,
I hope that I don't fail.
You'd think that they'd be
  very strong,
But they're fragile as can be,
To find one that's unbroken
Is a miracle to me.

poem: Ellen • illustration: Patricia

Time Change

All this messing with the clocks
Makes me kind of crazy
In the Spring I can't get up,
It makes me feel so lazy
In the Fall I'm wide awake,
An hour in advance,
I'd choose to never make the change
If I had the chance

poem: Ellen • illustration: Barbara

THIS 'N THAT

The Wish
Each birthday wish
I've ever had
Really does come true
Each year I wish
I'll grow some more
And every year I do
poem: Michele

Diversity
Diversity is good.
Many races, nationalities and religions
All in my neighborhood.
They are different,
Except in one way.
Like me they want their family
To be safe and happy
Every single day.
poem: Barbara and John
illustration: Barbara

Painting
Painting gives me time to think
It shows just who I am
It lets me say what's on my mind
So people understand
poem: Tom • illustration: Barbara

★ THIS 'N THAT ★

Look Up in the Sky

Look up in the sky
On a cloudy day.
Watch the fluffy puffy
Animals at play.
First a rabbit, then a duck,
And then a giant ray.
And just like that
They all drift away.

poem: Barbara and John

Playing My Trumpet

They tell me "Practice, practice!"
But it's hard to learn to play
I'm afraid if I don't get better
They'll take my horn away

poem: Alan • illustration: Patricia

Mermaids

Are mermaids real,
I really wonder?
Do they swim like a seal
And have to stay under?
Do they walk like me
When they are on land?
If they speak to me
Will I understand?
Are mermaids real,
I really wonder?

poem: John • illustration: Barbara

Playing Soccer

Two teams on the field
Running so quick it's like
    they soar.
Take that ball and kick,
Right into the goal and SCORE!

poem: Alexa • illustration: John

To Mrs. Kilian

By Meghan Miller

Second grade is long ago
But the memories are clear.
Your smiling face and open arms
Filled my days with cheer.

You made learning elementary topics
Interesting and fun,
While your poems on the chalkboard
Enlightened everyone.

Our young minds absorbed
Every single word you said,
And when I think back to those days now
A small yet special tear is shed.

Lucky for me we kept in touch
Long after my Wilson School days.
I looked forward to your summer postcards;
Your trips never ceased to amaze.

To my favorite teacher, Mrs. Kilian,
Although it's been quite a while,
My thoughts of you from second grade
Will always make me smile.

A Poem for My Teacher

By Taylor Khalil

A poem for my teacher
Who meant so much to me
Your passion, charisma, & warmth
Brought me so much joy

I'm grateful for your knowledge
& for the care you always showed
The poems you read to the class daily
Were the highlight of my mornings

I will never forget the smile on your face
As you greeted us at the door each day
Your classroom was warm and inviting
Just as you always were

Thank you, my teacher
For all you've done for me
I'll miss your postcards and your emails
But I know you're now at peace

Thank you for everything, Mrs. Kilian

Miss Alexa Lewis' Pre-school Student Art Contributions

Poems for all Ages

You can be five
You can be ninety-five
Poems will make
Your brain awake

This poem was written by Lou's friend, Ellen Haring, to help him and all Michele's family and friends work through their grief. It is comforting. Family members cherish the poem and perhaps you can share with someone you know who is grieving. Michele left us on January 22, 2022.

Grieving

By Ellen Haring
Illustration by Patricia Kilian

You're angry, hurt and, oh, so sad,
Your soul is sore and raw.
Not fair to lose someone you love—
The injustice of it all.

I know you've heard this all before,
That deep-felt ache will wane,
Just focus on good memories
And time will ease the pain.

Michele was full of life and joy,
She wants us all to thrive.
We honor her and work to keep
Her memory alive.

Made in United States
North Haven, CT
19 May 2022